Apple Mind

Katie Richards

Harbor Editions
Small Harbor Publishing

Apple Mind

Cover art: Sarah Jarrett, "The First Garden"
Cover design: Brianna Chapman
Interior design: Sarah Mengel
Editor: Greg Stapp
Small Harbor Executive Editor: Kristiane Weeks-Rogers
Small Harbor Publisher: Allison Blevins

APPLE MIND
KATIE RICHARDS
ISBN 978-1-957248-34-9
Harbor Editions,
an imprint of Small Harbor Publishing

Contents

Apple Mind

Language Acquisition through Motor Planning (LAMP)
Words for Life® Core Board

for
my love, S.R.

M-CHAT-R (Modified Checklist for Autism in Toddlers, Revised)

1. If you point at something across **THE** room, does your child look at it? (FOR EXAMPLE, if you **POINT** at a toy or an animal, does your child look at the toy or animal?)
2. Have you ever wondered if your child might be deaf?
3. Does your child play pretend or make-believe? (FOR EXAMPLE, pretend to drink from an empty cup, pretend to talk on a phone, or pretend to feed a doll or stuffed animal?)
4. Does your child like climbing on things? (FOR EXAMPLE, furniture, playground equipment, or stairs)
5. Does your child make unusual finger movements near his or her eyes? (FOR EXAMPLE, does your child wiggle his or her fingers to h**IS** or her eyes?) \
6. Does your child point with one finger **TO ASK FOR SOMETHING** or to get help? (FOR EXAMPLE, pointing to a snack or toy that is **OUT OF REACH**)
7. Does your child point with one finger to show you something interesting? (FOR EXAMPLE, pointing to an airplane in the sky or a big truck in the road. This is different from your child pointing to ASK for something [Question #6.])
8. Is your child interested in other children? (FOR EXAMPLE, does your child watch other children, smile at them, or go to them?)
9. Does your child show you things by bringing them to you or holding them up for you to see - not to get help, but just to share? (FOR EXAMPLE, showing you a flower, a stuffed animal, or a toy truck)
10. Does your child respond when you call his or her name? (FOR EXAMPLE, does he or she look up, talk or babble, or stop what he or she is doing when you call his or her name?)
11. When you smile at your child, does he or she smile back at you?
12. Does your child get upset by everyday noises? (FOR EXAMPLE, does your child scream or cry to noise such as a vacuum cleaner or loud music?)
13. Does your child walk?
14. Does your child look you in the eye when you are talking to him or her, playing with him or her, or dressing him or her

15. Does your child try to copy what you do? (FOR EXAMPLE, wave bye-bye, clap, or make a funny noise when you do)
16. If you turn your head to look at something, does your child look around to see what you are looking at?
17. Does your child try to get you to watch him or her? (FOR EXAMPLE, does your child look at you for praise, or say "look" or "watch me"?)
18. Does your child understand when you tell him or her to do something? (FOR EXAMPLE, if you don't point, can your child understand "put the book on the chair" or "bring me the blanket"?)
19. If something new happens, does your child look at your face to see how you feel about it? (FOR EXAMPLE, if he or she hears a strange or funny noise, or sees a new toy, will he or she look at your face?)
20. Does your child like movement activities? (FOR EXAMPLE, being swung or bounced on your knee)

§

Unfurl

Our boy, older now,
might remember

what I say.
And you're worried

about the daylilies
trimmed

by accident,
their roots webbing

through. What I want
to tell you is you

are not faultless
in this. You know

there's a reason I lose
my temper.

It's not caused by
our son's waking

as night breaks into day
and caterpillars bump

bump their bodies
across the sidewalk

to get picked
by mourning

doves. We
won't endure

ruin. Rhizomes

will grow un-

encumbered, body-
to-pillow. Our son rests

his face next to mine,
peaceful, asleep,

finally. This morning,
when he wakes, I will

redeem myself
in our garden.

We will have time
to watch roots

sprawl forward
to earth's heart,

a blessing. Leaves
will unfurl,

tender as
mice ears.

[apple]

You've had five today. You can have more tomorrow.

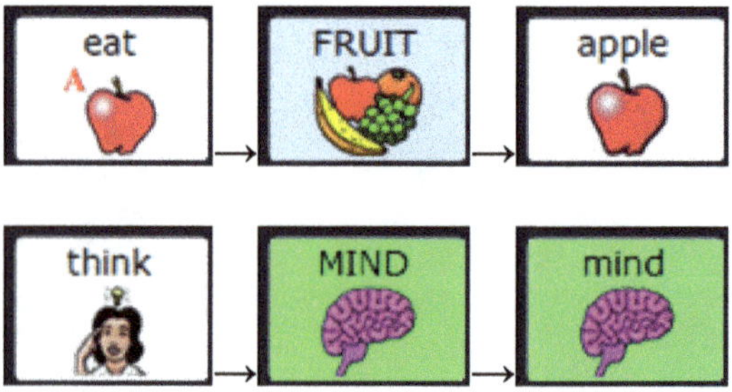

[apple mind]

You have apples on your mind?
Think about all the apples you'll have tomorrow.

[mean]

I'm not being mean. I don't want you to get a stomachache.

[mean apple want]

You mean you want another apple?
I promise, tomorrow you will get more apples.

How to Plant the Garden

Hack it up, the dirt I mean.

                                        Strike it
until you hit quartz with the shovel's edge.
Take care to preserve

                                        big fragments
if possible. These will be our seats and markers
and borders. Till it. Carry the

                                        unearthed
grass to the corner with no green,
fill the dearth. Water that spot.

                                        Rotate the earth,
add the fertile soil. The slow return
of earth to struck earth,

                                        the day
a cord pulled taut then slacked. Raise the bed sides up,
wood stacked and nailed.

                                        Gather the soil,
pile it high. We know nothing but earth
will have taught us, and we will

                                        trust her
until we have passed the day, we who never could
have dreamt it this way.
                                        How bold.

When you see my body

you don’t notice flat breasts
worn from two years of feeding,
the diastasis recti, the crooked front tooth,
half of my lip that doesn’t rise,
the squint in my left eye when I smile.
You see the curve of my shoulder,
perk of nipple in the chill
of the room, breadth of my back,
the space of it stretched between
my rib and heart, and the veins
of my breast, bloomed gerbera head
disk florets fluffed to seed, puffed sheep
sheared for wool pulled to yarn,
so soft, so warm, my thighs.

Glow Tender

i.

In the moment
of night's arrival,
when divorce
is mentioned,
we fuck harder,
hold our bodies
together then let go,
go to sleep angrier
and wake up
sorrier. I build a HAPPY
B-DAY DADDY banner
with the kids, punch
some holes into each paper
letter, run a ribbon through them,
hang the banner across the wall,
tape it, and re-tape it
until it stops falling
from its own weight.

ii.

Our knockout rose,
never pruned
correctly, grows
in its own pattern,
buds precious ovoids
of revival.

Name the center
where our toddler
receives his therapies.
I'll wait.
If I left tomorrow,
who would you call?

iii.

Belly pressed
to back, past
midnight,

rest your palm
on my thigh,
lace our

fingers together,
squeeze until
I can feel

the ache
of our bodies
as they

try to rest.
Your chest
falls and rises

under the sheets
overdue for
a washing.

We are tired,
so very tired.

iv.

When I bring up
divorce the night before
your birthday, what
I really want you to do
is name the center
where our boy gets
his care. I will
sing earth to you.

Oh, I will sing, sing,
sing to the body
of you. I have now
witnessed the shiver
of the willow oak
leaves, their edges
curled in. You
never scream back.

You walk away
instead. The late heat
of August, a breath
of night's peace.

v.

In the moonlight,
leaves drift, a sign

of summer's waning.
A cold wind crests

between the branches,
pulls them to the bellied earth.

A fog. The air manifests.
Where is the breath?

vi.

I want to see you
hold his AAC device
for him, learn the motor

plan of his words, and wait
for him to attempt to speak
before stepping in to teach him

the location of his words.
I need you to tell me
you see me, you appreciate

my efforts. I need you to acknowledge
how important this communication
work is. What if I gave you

a glimpse 3 years from now?
Are you here when our boy, still
non-speaking, asks me:

[Am I you?]

vii.

The rose bush stands
against the moonless sky,

its thorns silhouetted
against the tender

glow of the porch light
this night, its new buds

delectable, full,
its branches artery

the place in the sky
that will once again hold

the sun. It is promised to us.
It is ours to claim.

viii.

A rose bloom
punches through sepal,
a shoulder pulled
from its socket.

Cerise sky, glorious gasp,
the fall of day into night,
the clasp of a bracelet
released, the clouds spread

thin. My mouth to yours,
I give a little love.
You are my paper doll,
and I pick you up,

caress you before
shredding you, your form
piled before me,
a mountained stillness.

ix.

A bullfrog's
throat swells,
its scream
resounds. Water
in a glass bumped.
The stars vibrate.

x.

Buds heaven up.
Fingers reach out-
stretched from each other.
The breath of atmosphere
woven between them—
thorn doily—

center peaked
as a cathedral steeple.
Feel the breath of
fall on this, this last
gasp of summer,
dew weaving itself

into the bed of grass.
We will feel the shift
in the dew from humid
to startling chill
and our bodies
will know it. O, sing

with me, please. Name it and
hold me as fall breaks its form
into us, its first breath enters us
in the evenings where heat
leaves the leaves, and the chill
dries everything to crisp.

Divorce Aubade

We pause to hear birds
chatter the world to wake.

We listen while holding hands
in bed, talk, our fingers

woven together. I am worried.
You are not. We've had a long year,

how can you be so sure? We love each other,
that hasn't changed. Our hearts

knock rhythmic like the dip of the humming-
bird's beak in and out of the neighbor's feeder.

WHAT

IS

DIFFICULT

VARIES

THE

MORE

I SEPARATE

FROM

YOU

Your word repetitions are patterns.
Patterns can make a poem.

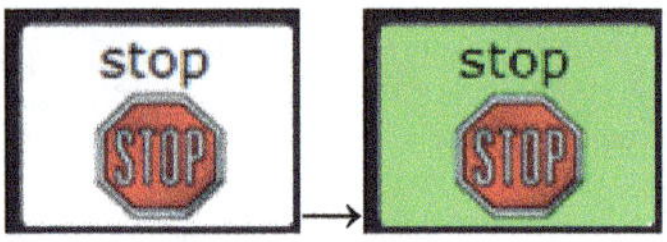

[stop]

Your patterns aren't poems?

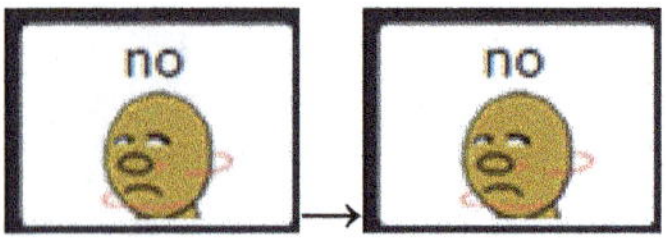

[no]

Oh, ok. I'll stop calling them poems.

Shake You

the irises their centers white
edges deep violet these petals

predictable like clockwork
each April just as the gladioli in July

they come and I have no idea why
or how they keep tune to Earth's

turning and we hold ourselves
to these patterns and don't let

the stuttering of things shake us
the ridges underneath mushrooms

ordered lines predictable
as the lines in the ribs of carcasses

picked clean by vultures the pull
of their wings in front of them

unfurled to heaven their wings' force
lifts them lets them script across the sky

lines above
    lines above

This garden

borders our porch, faces
south where the sun beats down.

There rests the trellis, the honeysuckle
vining itself along. Fragrant honeysuckle—

the smell of it heavy, dense, the drape
of wind before a thunderstorm, honey-

suckle mouth opened, a low o, vines scrolled, the fold
of a wrist around a waist, leaves woven into space.

We will see the light glitter through the open space
leaves cleft, and, when we are thirsty, we will lift

the trumpets, feel the purse of petal
soft as silt, blare nectar to tongue.

This garden

is not the place where we doubt where we spread hate where we shout and I scream fuck you you fucking fucker when you tell me to stop swearing in front of the kids not the place where we go to bed actually fuck then get up for church the next morning to be blessed

Pollinate

I rest my palm
on your shoulder,

let it fall away
in sleep. The world

between us
is a bloom set

to collapse. Digger
wasps curl their

abdomens under,
flitter their stingers,

twist their feet
around the blooms

of the knockout
out front. Flicker

of their feet, little
thumbs fiddling.

On the stoop lies
a dahlia picked

then dropped,
its petals dried

in place. I move

my hand towards you

only to take it back.
Our girl plucks

the clover from
under the bees,

lays the blooms
before me only

to gather them back,
drops the stems

one by one.
Bees return to

blooms. A busy
humming. Our boy

catches them then
releases them,

a small danger,
his opened fingers

the firework
bursts they spark

out of. The flowers
we picked last week

start to rot. I dump
the vase, hope I have

caught them
in time to dry

open. Your hand
finds mine

under the sheets,

your thumb paused

to my wrist.
This pulse

our moment.
My hand rests

against your chest.
We are but a gasp.

I can feel
within you,

a rhythm steady.
The marigolds

hold their color
best. When you

ask me, *Do you
even like me*

anymore? I say,
No, not really,

and then pause

before I clarify,

*I'm not saying that
out of anger either.*

You pause
before you say,

I know. That

makes it worse.

The lavender
sprigs dry

a purple pale,
the type of purple

that makes you
squeeze your

hands under your
knees and ache

for the return
of spring. Wasps

pollinate, too.
But we still

kill them. I'm not
used to hearing that

sort of waver
in your voice.

Solidago quivers
against the road,

a gold thrash
ushering fall in.

We are foolish,
I think. But when

we are this tired
and depleted,

we have done
our best. Tickseeds

whorl borders
to the road,

a shimmer beautiful.
You leave

and come back
with one for me,

root ball held
in a grocery bag.

The tickseed
transplants easily

to the garden,
sits loud

against the house,

a yellow slap

against the gray
siding. In and out

of its blossoms,
the wasps flicker.

Solidago

You: a breath of August,
the spark of summer

panicled to end. Teensy
flowerets, let me run

my fingers through you,
brush your golden petals

against my cheek. Let me
watch pipevine swallowtails come

rest on you, lift their tongues,
raise your nectar.

Taste it. Let me
watch them still

their wings. Blue ends
drop like rain, flutter

in the blooms
open and ready to hymn them.

§

Invocate

i.

Picture with me this garden bed
with spots of dearth, the dust
of earth jaspered to our soles.
What a long summer
Our Father who art in heaven,
but finally we have a handle
on our son's diagnosis *hallowed*
be Thy name. The path of grass
behind furled from our walking
Thy kingdom, pattern swirled to center,
a mini universe, its throat
calling me *come Thy will.* Flowing
as milk, this honeysuckle renders
the wood line sweet, delicate,
rain caught in the funnel
spider's web.

Tell me, what is it
we have
gained? Sun's
glow hems us. Take
my hand, the warmth
of body stretched over
body. And, like the fold
of the grass *be done,*
we weave to one another.

ii.

In our garden
there are

no appointments
no therapies

when we see
our daughter

stimming
no need

to start interventions
when we finish

returning earth
to earth shifted

you place your hand
on earth as it is

in heaven under
my chin

rhododendron
leaves perk

to the sun
give us this

day as we watch
the garter snake

poke its body

out cautious

slow *our daily*
bread on earth

an energy
spread quiet

the sun through
the trees

iii.

I have nothing left
to give to you,

and I am sorry
for the words I said

and forgive us
our sins in our exhaustion.

But I am most sorry
for the truth in them.

iv.

Oak twig
floats through

the river's
rhythm pushes

its golden leaf
forward a fall

crown rolls
to current

then pops back
up curled

a golden hand
gives the benediction

as we forgive
you would think

the regression
wouldn't have

surprised me
with our second

but once again
I find myself

asking when
was the last time

our child called

me *mama*

I can't tell you or
I would've held her

calling to me
a little closer

v.

I take her to the appointment alone because we've done this before and we know what to expect. You come home with a burrito from my favorite restaurant and sit by me on the couch. I am spent, so you hold my hand while I eat. We talk about the word *diagnosis*, how its sense of dread and disease doesn't feel right. I tear up only when we discuss the burden of parenting two neurodiverse children in an unaccommodating world, and *those who sin against us* the next day I call for the referrals to start her therapies. We share the news with family and friends and wince when we receive condolence after condolence. We aren't grieving.

vi.

Early morning, trill
your light over us *and lead*
us not as you clamor your glory.

A tender pulling of dew
to blade's surface. Walk with me
into temptation on this path born new.

And remember how we oathed
each other to have and to
hold and to hold and to hold and

to hold and to hold and what
of that oath? My form to your form
deliver us, the shudder of your breath

through mine, glass blown *for thine*
is the kingdom, and we are the moment
and the power and the glory of this day's

breaking. The wind *forever*
and ever, a whish, mouths our hair,
the blades, a buttercup.
Amen.

When I call you by name, you no longer

Field of Flowers, Purcellville, VA

look up little
darling look
up from the dahlia

you hold its stem
so close so
large so

sideways so
you can look
at the light

glow green
through its
hollow

TEACH

ME

YOUR

NEEDS

[miss]

What do you miss?

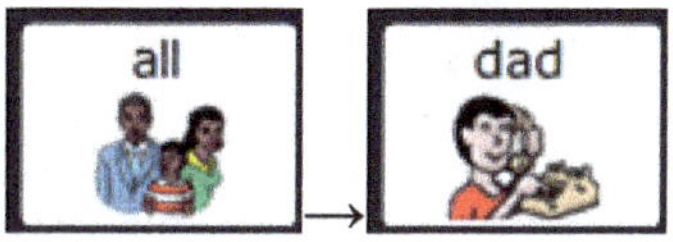

[dad]

I'm sorry you miss Daddy. He's working late tonight.

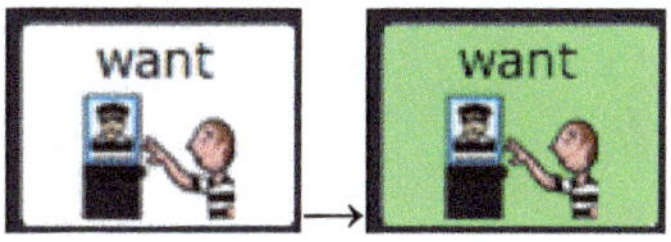

[want]

What do you want?

[hug my dad]

The Edge of God

Violets wild
their presence
across this god-
damn yard we never
could control. Regret
is body, is verdure
fading. Blooms
choke out each
seed we toss.
In the corner,
under the cover
of the live oak,
rests a larkspur
forgotten.

Prayer of Self-Offering

lodged stalks
split in the middle

the eye of a needle
the wind threads

through let us sing
let us wander

this failed harvest
and gather what

belongs to us
the clouds

swirled and lifted
my chin to heaven

I wonder what holds us
you and I are woven

as the wheat chaff
the rain falls

hard
it flowers

the earth
the field

floods to brown

the stretch

of body
tugged forward

the suck of
mud on foot

In the Corner of our Garden a Maple

its leaves
their blather
the twist
of their edges
their scent
bold and
earthy
bodies
impish
red shook
magic fall
saturation
saturation
ceaseless
wind blows
a whistle
through

EVEN
IN
OUR
HARD TIME

I

CARE
FOR

YOU

[he hopes divorce]

Don't say that. Daddy and I love each other.

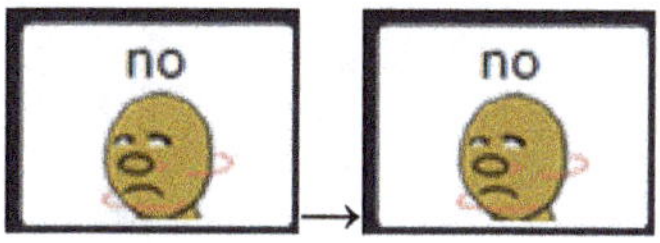

[no]

Yes, we do. Sometimes we yell and say things we don't mean.

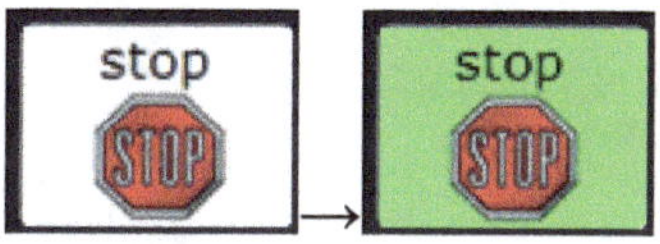

[stop]

Constellations

Even though we have no need
for sleep in our garden, we will

still have night and the stars will shine
bright. And the constellations—

the constellations, can I tell you? Mapping
our children's words across their AAC devices

has taught us how to tap our fingers across
the stars, galaxies motor-planned to meaning.

We will learn to speak in the tongues
of the heavens, and there will we whisper

our secrets to each other, let the moon-
glow marvel into our garden bed,

and you will trace the glint of it into
my form as cicadas cry us their lullabies.

Wildflower Sketches

frost aster
arms
raised above
your head
you watch
me pull
off my
top with
the little
hole forming
by the pocket
your shoulders
circle out
the length
of your arms
short in
proportion
to your
body

tall hairy
no pun
intended
though
you are
both
fragile
bloom
yellow
head
thrown
back
legs and
arms out
stretched
on the bed

southern barren strawberry
how sparkle
right
your eyes
the lashes
long
this a slip
of heaven
brought to
dermis
when you
slip lip
to neck
lift light
to my
collarbone

scarlet beebalm
and sometimes
your eyebrow
hairs they
grow wily
and I run
my mouth
across them
kiss you
gently
lie with me
here your palm
on my belly
the warmth
a starburst
the universe
is pulling
its moment
in through
the sacrum
and I have
a little space
between
my thighs
a little more
and a sigh

least bluet
brown iris
pupil round

bulbous buttercup
the cupping
of your
hand over
my breast
turned
your body
to me
pressed

cornflower
an expanse
the glow
and we
will O O

Hummingbird

shingles staggered how shine
          your feathers
glitter their luster

panes of glass
stained shimmer little
bubbles blown

through wand to orb
the sun it takes its lessons
from your glitter its vigor

Sialia Sialis

island   the eye
          head blue   see

earth feathered into sea
copper birthed softer

a wing is a cup is a

          snatch of wind
          pushed under chest
          eucharist is this

          bread
          breath
          breadth

an island an eye a body blown to sea

Heart Nerve Anatomy

Your lips,
curved cathedral
nave, I am here
to worship,

to say my prayers,
to give a benediction.
My lips trail
the space

between
your chest.
My palm maps
the veins

of pipevine wings
beating in your
lungs. Your arms
around me:

Invocation
is this.

When raptors kettle

what can we do but look up
at the red-tailed hawks

their swoop and weave an infinite
pause your breath against me

this gap between our hands
collapsed thin their wings

shadow the frozen field
lines above lines their forms

distant then close the expansion
of the ribs after an inhalation

the expanse of your hand
meets the breadth of my palm

Reclamation

Lichen spots the willow oak,
bare branches spread out
like nerve endings. We haven't
raked at all this year. Leaves lie
ungathered, their curled forms
softened by the snow. The snow,
it covers everything. Today
is a quiet day. How amazing
then is our girl's cry when
I walk away. Her *Mama*
breaks the silence.

WHAT is autism spectrum disorder (ASD)?

*Autism spectrum disorder (ASD) **IS** a developmental disorder. It affects a person's behavior and makes communication and social interactions **DIFFICULT**. *ASD can range from mild to severe. The type of symptoms a person has and how severe they are **VARIES**. Some children may not be able to function without a lot of help from parents and other caregivers. O**THE**rs may develop social and verbal skills and lead independent lives as adults. *Most people with ASD will always have some trouble communicating or interacting with others. But early diagnosis and treatment have helped **MORE** and more people who have ASD lead full lives and do things such as going to college and having a job. *ASD now includes conditions that used to be d**I**agnosed **SEPARATE**ly. These include autism, Asperger's syndrome, pervasive developmental disorder, and childhood disintegrative disorder. Any of these terms might still be used by you or your doctor to describe your condition.

What causes ASD?

*The exact cause of ASD is not known. *False claims in the news have made some parents concerned about a link between ASD and vaccines. But studies have found no link between vaccines and ASD. It's important to make sure that your child gets all childhood vaccines. They help keep your child **FROM** getting serious diseases that can cause harm or even death.

What increases the risk of ASD?

*ASD tends to run in families, so experts think it may be something that **YOU** inherit. Scientists are trying to find out exactly which genes may be responsible for passing down ASD in families. ASD tends to occur more often in people who have certain genetic conditions. These may include fragile X syndrome and tuberous sclerosis. *Some things increase the chance that you'll have a baby with ASD. These things are called risk factors. The risk of having a baby with ASD is higher if either birth parent: Is at an older age, Has another child who has ASD, Has a family history of learning problems.

How is it treated?

*The goals of treatment for ASD are to: Reduce ASD symptoms and Support learning and development at home and in school. *Treating ASD early gives you the tools and support to help your child lead the best life possible. *What type of treatment your child may need depends on the symptoms. These are different for each child. And treatment may change over time. Because people with ASD are so different, something that helps one person may not help another. Work with everyone involved in your child's education and care to find the best way to help manage symptoms and help your child thrive to the best of his or her ability. *Treatment may include: Behavioral training and management–this approach rewards appropriate behavior (positive reinforcement) to teach children social skills and to **TEACH** them how to communicate and how to help themselves as they grow older. And this approach teaches you how to work with your child at ho**ME** and to help **YOUR** child practice new skills; Specialized therapies, depending on your child's **NEEDS**–these may include speech and occupational therapy; Medicine–it might be used to treat symptoms of ASD, such as irritability and hyperactivity. Sometimes medicine is also used to treat other problems such as anxiety, depression, or obsessive-compulsive behaviors.

How can your family cope with having a child who has ASD?

*An important part of your child's treatment plan is to make sure that other family members get training about ASD and how to help manage symptoms. Training can reduce family stress and help your child function better. Some families need more help than others.

Take advantage of every kind of help you can find. Talk to your doctor about what help is available where you live. Family, friends, public agencies, and ASD organizations are all possible resources.

Remember these tips:

- Educate yourself about ASD. Learning all you can about ASD can help you know how to help your child develop independence.
- Plan breaks. The daily demands of caring for a child with ASD can take their toll. Planned breaks will help you

connect with others in your family or have time for yourself.

- Make time for an activity you enjoy, **EVEN** if you can only do it for a few m**IN**utes each day.
- Get extra help when y**OUR** child gets older. The teen years can be a very **HARD TIME** for children with ASD. Community services and public programs can help.
- Get in touch with other families who have children with ASD. You can talk about your problems and share advice with people who will understand.
- Plan for your child's future. As your child gets older, th**I**nk about where your adult child will live and what training and employment resources he or she may need. Also, take steps to ensure that your adult child will have proper **CARE** and resources throughout life. Find out if your child is eligible **FOR** assistance.
- Focus on your child's strengths. Like any other child, **YOU**r child has strengths and weaknesses. Help build those strengths by encouraging your child to explore interests at home and in school.

THE
POINT

IS
TO ASK FOR
SOMETHING
OUT OF REACH

eat
FRUIT
apple
want
want
please
please
get
get
eat
FRUIT
apple
want
want
said
COMMUNI
communic
eat
hungry

Acknowledgments

Minspeak® and LAMP Words for Life® are registered trademarks of Prentke Romich Company. © 2024 PRC-Saltillo. Images used with permission. All rights reserved.

"The point" is an erasure of the M-CHAT-R autism screening test for toddlers.

"What is difficult" is an erasure of Kaiser Permanente's "Autism Spectrum Disorder" Topic Overview website that we were sent after each child's diagnosis. https://wa.kaiserpermanente.org/kbase/topic.jhtml?docId=hw152184

If you want to learn more about how to support and respect those who use AAC, the Communication Bill of Rights is a helpful resource that can be found on the ASHA site: https://www.asha.org/njc/communication-bill-of-rights/

Special thanks and appreciation, in no specific order, to the following:

Ms. Bethany, for loving my family and teaching us AAC. My family couldn't have started this journey towards communication without you.

Ms.A, Ms.B, Ms.C, Ms.G, Mr.J, Ms.K, Ms.K, Mr.M, Ms.N, Ms.S, and Ms.T my family is forever grateful to you all. It truly takes a community.

To the non-profit CommunicationFIRST for teaching me all that I don't know and helping me become a better ally to my AAC users.

To my family, always, for your continued support in my writing endeavors and the joy and laughter you bring to my life.

To my poetry family—Buffy, Chike, Jonah, and Marion—much love and appreciation to you all for helping me revise many of these poems and keeping me writing every week. XOXO

To my teachers, mentors, and friends—Jen, Sally, and Eric—thank you for all you have taught me and the support you have given me over the years to see this book to fruition.

To my dear friends—Amy, Carrie, Ella, Elissa, Jenn, Sarah, Siobhan, and Xandra—thank you for being my biggest cheerleaders and reading drafts when needed.

To the Tupelo Manuscript Conference—thank you Kristina Marie Darling and Jeffrey Levine for the close care and assistance you gave me in tightening this book.

To the editors at Harbor Editions, thank you, *thank you*, for believing in this work and giving me the opportunity to bring this book into the world.

Katie Richards' (she/her) debut collection, *Apple Mind,* was selected as an editors' pick for the Laureate Prize with Harbor Editions. It was also a semi-finalist for the 2021 Philip Levine Prize for Poetry. Her poetry has previously appeared in *Valparaiso Poetry Review*, *Harbor Review*, *DIALOGIST*, *Softblow*, *South Dakota Review*, and *Sweet Tree Review* among other places. Read more of her work at katie-richards.com and connect with her on Instagram and TikTok @katierichardspoet.

About Small Harbor Publishing

Small Harbor Publishing is a 501c3 nonprofit organization. Our goal is to publish unique and diverse voices. We are a feminist press, and we are committed to diversity and inclusion. We strive to bring new voices to a devoted and expanding readership.

Small Harbor Publishing began in 2018 with the first issue of *Harbor Review*. The magazine is an online space where poetry and art converse. *Harbor Review* quickly grew and now publishes reviews and runs multiple micro chapbook competitions, including the Washburn Prize and the Editor's Prize.

In July 2020, Small Harbor Publishing was officially incorporated and began Harbor Editions. Harbor Editions accepts submissions through a chapbook open reading period, a hybrid chapbook open reading period, the Marginalia Series, and the Laureate Prize.

In 2023, Harbor Anthologies began with a mission to promote texts that explore social justice issues and highlight marginalized writers.

If you would like to support Small Harbor Publishing, please visit our "About" page at smallharborpublishing.com/about.

www.ingramcontent.com/pod-product-compliance
Lightning Source LLC
Chambersburg PA
CBHW062120080426
42734CB00012B/2925
* 9 7 8 1 9 5 7 2 4 8 3 4 9 *